Vibr:

Healthy and Powerful Living

(Book Three)

Dr. Josefina Monasterio

What Others Have to Say

Josefina is one of the happiest, healthiest, and most well-rounded individuals I have met in my life. She is an immigrant from Venezuela, she obtained a PhD in the United States, and she devotes her life to supporting the health and fitness of others, and to spreading the word that it is possible to say strong, fit and healthy even while the birthdays continue to accumulate.

Wow, I love how you constantly reinvent yourself for the better. Thanks for sharing a little about the beginning of your life. I know sometimes we don't like to recall poor experiences but it helps to glorify The Lord and how he brought us a mighty long way. Plus going through the fires of life helps to create and shape who we become. Our challenges are God designed to build integrity within as he creates the Diamonds that we become! Thanks again for sharing, and I love your new website. POW!

Josefina, a favorite part of my day is your way of helping us start the day. It is beautiful and empowering! I appreciate you greatly. I am also looking forward to reading your books. I will purchase them as a birthday present to myself to celebrate my 71st birthday. God bless you.

Today is the beginning of my life and I am really living it. I was meant to cross paths with you, and I am so very thankful for this, more than you will ever know. God bless you. POW!

I gave birth to my beautiful daughter at the age of 36. I want to be around to watch her reach adulthood and beyond. You are such an inspiration to help me do that. Since following you I've changed my lifestyle and everyone notices the difference. Thank you. C.R.

Josefina, I dreamed I met you last night. I was thrilled! I went on and on telling you what you have done for me through your books and social media! I have a completely focused mindset with your help. I'm going to crush my goals. God bless you. J.W.

I used to struggle getting up in the mornings because of my lack of physical, mental, and spiritual health. I can honestly say you are helping me transform. I look forward to scriptures and beach time with you each day.

JO! I had never read your slogan, *Give yourself the opportunity to fail*! That is so powerful, and true. The American culture ridicules failure, but to get to new levels you have to fail. What a wise saying.

AMAZING ! I think this woman is a real peek into our evolution. It is happening now. Old age wears an extremely different look than it did 40-50 years ago. You would never have seen a 71 year old woman live and look like that. D.A.

I only have a couple of pages to finish reading your book. I love it. I will start incorporating all of these good habits to fit my lifestyle and begin a journey of feeling great, happy and healthy!

I love that you love God and proclaim it so humbly. You are such a precious soul. Thank you for all you do so freely for your fellow brothers and sisters. You are a true disciple.

I follow your videos and chats and am putting everything into practice. Today I cleaned my Facebook page of all negative people.

I'm 32 and recently joined my husband in the gym. Heart disease and failure run in my family, which is my main reason for joining. I was surprised that I enjoyed it so much. I look forward to going every time! I'm still new and not sure if I'm doing enough to push myself, but I'm sure it's better than doing nothing. Anyway, I just wanted to tell you I think you are an inspiration for women of all ages. You look incredible!

Wow, very inspiring. You give me hope as a mom at 55, with a three-year-old and eight-year-old, that I can get my body fit again. I lost my groove; taking care of myself is hugely lacking; I need to unpack 40 pounds. You give me hope - inside and out - to do it. I need to keep as healthy as possible, inside and out, as my hubby and I want to be around for our kids. Praying up. K.

Fantastic! is what you have done for me physically and spiritually. I'm 68 and am inspired by you. In the eight months I've worked at it I lost four inches and nearly 40 lbs; I feel great: great energy, dance, etc.

ISBN-13: 978-1719472685

Vibrant at Any Age series

Book One: *Vibrant at Any Age: A guide to renew your life and become vigorous, healthy, and happy* (English and Spanish editions)

Book Two: *Vibrant Learning: Developing and Perfecting Yourself* (English and Spanish editions)

Book Three: *Vibrant Relationships for Healthy and Powerful Living*

You can reach Dr. Josefina at DrJosefinaMonasterio@gmail.com

Website: www.DrJosefina.com
Facebook: www.facebook.com/drjosefina
Twitter: www.twitter.com/drjosefina
YouTube: www.youtube.com/drjosefina

Contents

PREFACE

This is my third book in the series *Vibrant at Any Age*. Each has to do with taking control of your life so it is you who decides how to age, not the culture, not your doctor, not your friends. This book focuses on relationships because when it's all said and done the only thing that lasts in this life—and continues on into the next—are the people you genuinely care about and those who care about you.

As I write this book I am thinking of you, wanting the best *you* to come forth. And I appreciate your prayers and well wishes for me in return. I care about you because you are the brothers and sisters of my extended family. While we may not be near physically, in spirit there is no separation. That's why when I send you a kiss, it's more real than you can imagine.

INTRODUCTION

We are not born to be alone. As it is written, "It is not good that the man should be alone; I will make him an help meet for him" (Genesis 2:18). There is an innate urge to share our lives with others. We stimulate one another to grow and become more than we are. That's why it's so important to have loving relationships; they create, they change you, and they change the world.

Having a good relationship depends on freely expressing what's deeply embedded from birth, the real you. Relationships suffer when you are unreal. The antidote? Sincerity, more sincerity, and greater sincerity, without which no relationship can flourish.

While we are born with undesirable inclinations from our heredity, we also inherit God's DNA. As we interact with negativity in our environment—people, places, and things—we form an image of ourselves that separates us from God who is our real father. The image we identify with is based on the ideas, experiences, and opinions of others. As a consequence, our decisions are determined by how the world has programmed us, and not God's plan for us.

We are created for excellence
but the world programs us for failure

So how do we resolve this awful condition? That's what this book is about so you can enter into wonderful and fulfilling relationships, with those close to you and those you chance to meet as you pass by.

But be ever mindful that the most powerful relationship we will ever have is our divine relationship with God. Happy hour is hanging out with him.

GOD AND RELATIONSHIPS

I use my physical body to extol and glorify God.
As he says, the body is the temple of the Holy Spirit.

I am going to tell you right off that there is nothing more important in a relationship than your spiritual life. Being a good person, being kind and all that goes with it starts here. It begins with your relationship with your Heavenly Father, from which everything trickles down. If I want to live and work well with others, I must first live and work well with God in my life. What do I mean by this? Your relationships can grow only so much if you haven't made it the business of your life to find out who is guiding you and then cooperate with him.

It is more than just knowing *about* him. It requires hearing the still small voice of his Spirit Presence within. He is your Creator Parent, which is why you want to talk things over with him. And it's not just big things, but it's what you do all the time, like what should I eat and where should I go?

I strive to be in touch with God all the time. My antenna is always out and receiving. This enables him to download into me what I need to thrive. The download usually takes place during my Morning Ritual.

I call hanging out with God and watching the sunrise
Rise and Shine.

As God downloads his love, thoughts, and wisdom, I upload my willingness to follow his instructions; it's a two-way street. It's

4

about being friends with God in a very real way, like you would with your closest buddy. It's the most important thing in life.

For me God is Energy that's the way I experience His Power. He gave me a unique portion of his personality. It's why I am who I am and you are who you are. It is why I can relate to my Father person to person. I talk with him and he talks with me.

I realize that many do not know our Creator this way. For those who recognize there is something up there in charge of everything but are unsure of what it is, you can try thinking of God as the Divine Presence in your life, always trying to guide you to the best place you can be. It will help you immensely to learn the soft touch of his hand and trust the still-small-voice of his Spirit. Then all things work out for the best. Guaranteed!

In summary, the most important relationship we can have is our relationship with our loving heavenly Father. It's where our true identity comes from. Then the purpose and plan for our lives become clear and easier to cooperate with. When you do your homework of getting to know him and develop an intimate relationship, you experience the kingdom of heaven on earth. Although the world of the spirit is invisible, it is nonetheless real when you are connected to it. That's when you experience what the scripture says, "All things work together for good to them that love God." The miracles that happen every day when you live a God-centered life will delight you.

Where it all begins

It's best if two people are on the same page spiritually. For example, an atheist and a God-centered person can get only so close in their marriage or partnership (this applies to business as well). There will be a barrier you cannot get beyond. You can grow only so close and the relationship can go only so far if two people are mismatched spiritually. It's like trying to plow a field with a horse and a donkey; it doesn't work.

You may be physically compatible, you may think alike about many things, you may even share the same sense of what's right and wrong. But if you don't share a belief in God, you get only so close and bam! you hit a stone wall. There is a dissonance, a noise always in the background upsetting things.

You can read all the self-help books you want, go to psychologists, and it won't help. You may even think alike, but because there is discord on the spiritual level, separation is built in; there is a gulf you cannot cross.

People do not click and they wonder why. I'm not talking about theological differences. You can have a Christian and a Muslim, a Jew and a Hindu, and it will be fine if they both want to find their Divine Source, discover his purpose for them, and be guided by it. That unifies people more than anything else. There is an attraction, a gravity pull, between the spirit nature of persons with such similar longings—thus the term "kindred spirits."

There is greatness seeded in each of us by our Creator Parent. The goodness within you is yearning to come forth. It is up to you to provide the favorable conditions to make it happen. What are these conditions?

- Belief, faith, and trust in your connection to a higher source. I hate to tell you atheists that you can go only so far by self-will and willpower. Although you can accomplish much, the energy of the higher dimension remains closed to you.
- The desire to express the real you, to let her come out fearlessly. Follow the career designed for you from eternity.
- Your focus on discerning the divine will and acting on it. The practical aspect translates into loving others and going about doing good—service, more service, and greater service.

- Develop your intuitive sense that accesses the deepest recesses of your heart and the portal of your higher mind. Learn to trust in the still-small-voice.
- Be patient with yourself. It is a daily walk by which you release the greatness (goodness) within you.

Unify with God

It's important to be connected so when God downloads his will you recognize, receive, and act on it. But how do you get connected? It's difficult for many people because this world is so material-minded; the spiritual part of life is hazy and mysterious. Furthermore, we're not raised to develop our intuitive sense and trust in our hearts. What do I mean by trusting in your heart? It was explained to me this way: there is a fragment of God given to each of us who lives within the temple of our hearts. He's literally there—but imprisoned—as he waits on us to turn the key and release him that he may guide us.

It begins with inviting God to share your inner life, from where creativity, joy, and happiness originate. It's best done consciously, a wholehearted consecration that changes your life. You dedicate to making choices based on spiritual insight and divine guidance. After you have done this, here are a few things you can practice each day to open the cell door wide. Remember that you are training your spiritual muscles the same way you train your physical muscles at the gym.

You want to have an intimate relationship with your best friend, so hang out with God from the beginning of your day. As soon as you wake up, smile and thank him. Ask him, *What do you want me to do?* Read the scriptures (or whatever source of spiritual truth you feel good about), study and memorize them, imprint them in your heart, pray, and meditate. Feel the connection, the warmth of that loving sweet Presence in your life, your Creator, your friend. He is here with you right now. Fill your heart with gratitude and thankfulness. Feel the love and then go about your day.

This is what I call my Daily Ritual.

When you are disconnected

Jesus said, "My peace I give to you, but not as the world gives." What does the world offer? Drugs, pornography, alcohol, endless rounds of therapy—and yet we are still missing what we seek. I see it all the time with my clients. They don't know that the peace they are searching for only God can provide.

Jesus continued, "Let not your heart be troubled, neither let it be afraid." In other words, don't allow yourself to be agitated and disturbed; do not permit yourself to be fearful, intimidated, cowardly, and unsettled. When you commit to developing an intimate relationship with God, you get it all. And you now have the best life coach in the universe.

WOW, what a promise! What a therapy!

Here's how it works. As soon as the angels see you looking within, your celestial friends come near and more effectively participate in the events of your life; they provide the guidance, protection, and learning you need.

How often we fail to see the spirit at work in our lives because we are material minded. That narrow vision brings trouble. When it happens to me, Psalm 23 calms me where it says, "He makes me lie down." What does it take to remind yourself of your place in the Father's heart? Find out what works for you. As soon as you feel separated, stop right away and go to your spiritual savings account and withdraw the credits you need to reconnect.

Sometimes I am unsure; is it God's will or mine, Josefina the divine or Josefina the human? When I don't take the time to think if it's what he wants me to do, and just do what I feel like, that's when I get in trouble. Now this could be a learning experience if you rise above it and see it as God does. Say to yourself, *It didn't feel right. Let me go back to where I got derailed and learn from it so I don't lose my way again. I'll change direction and get back on track.*

How to reconnect

You win by learning

I never lose because I learn when I am disconnected. It's a win-win situation. If I whack you on the side of the head once, when I try the second time don't you duck? Why? Because we learn from experience.

When I need to reconnect I do what I call flashbacks. We have all had experiences with people who helped us with different situations. Get some quiet time and begin visualizing how things worked out in the past. Call to mind how your Spirit guided, cared for, and brought you to the place where you needed to be. These memories are where I go to encourage myself when something bad happens to me. I review how I overcame previous problems. It gives me the confidence that I am able to overcome this difficulty also. This is a good reason to look back; otherwise, be careful about living in the past.

Here's an example of a valuable experience that is now part of my memory bank: when I lived in Venezuela and how I escaped my poverty—a shack then but a "mansion" now.

Before   After

Memories have a tendency to fade as you live more in the present moment. When the issues that clung to me from the past were resolved, the negative force that anchored them left; the dark energy was no longer there to be irritated and aroused. The same can happen to anyone. As you correct the errors of your past a future unfolds with new possibilities of learning and progress.

It's worth repeating. Knowing where you came from buoys your faith that your current problems will also get resolved. If God got me out of that, what is too difficult for him? It takes faith, and then doing the work. It's like having an emotional savings account to draw upon when you need it. I have deposited all the things the Lord has done for me since I was five years old. It's actually a joint account. When I decide on the right thing to do, it is like putting in one dollar and God then puts in two. He gives you double for your trouble. The more you obey what he wants for you the more he puts into your account. He does everything abundantly. That is why my faith is strong. It's why I don't doubt, although I have my little trials here and there.

Things won't work out if you look to the world to answer your problems. The solutions you need come from your inner life. When I look back and see all the things God has done for me, I know that is not me doing them. He worked in my life back then and he will continue to make things happen now.

You get what you need

Every morning I say to God, *Let me know your will so I can do it*. Freely giving your will is the only gift you can give to your Creator, the only thing of value you have to offer. After all, he does have everything, so what else can you give him? This is genuine love because you cannot force someone to love you; it must be freely given.

God then provides whatever you need to fulfill your consecration. All the money you need, all the education you need, all the housing you need. Why? Because you told him, not my will, but yours. How else can you do his work if you don't have what you need?

Here I am at 72 years old, active on social media, talking about taking control of your life. Well, I live in a material world and I need a suitable place to live, wholesome food to eat, a dependable car to drive, and so on. God provides these things so I can follow his guidance and be an example of how to take control of your life.

If you're living on the street in a cardboard box, how is that going to work? Although people in that situation can choose to do God's will, it's much harder because they're so bogged down just getting enough to eat and a place to sleep. Poverty does not work well when you consecrate your will to him, which is why God will guide you out of that terrible situation and make you to lie down in green pastures.

I have enough self-respect when he provides the things I need that I don't say, "I don't deserve that." No! God loves me, I'm his child, he wants the best for me. God blows me away with how he provides everything in my life. What a delight he is, and clever too how he makes it all work out!

Many believe in God and expect him to provide what they need, and they are right. But it's your effort to hear and speak with him that enlarges your capacity to receive the blessings he has for you.

God's says to me, *I want you to prosper*. But I must believe that he means what he says. Then my trust and confidence in him can't help but say, *How wonderfully you work in my life. How great thou art!* That's how I praise him. When you live this way you experience the outpouring of his favor, blessing, and grace. I call it walking in the kingdom 24/7.

An example of being led

I love my Mitsubishi (car), as I love everything thing God gives me. As he says, every good gift comes from above. I do not take it for granted and respect what he provides, so I took good care of my Mitsubishi.

Suddenly I began sensing little things about my car, enough to think that God has something new for me. I said, *Hmm, God I think we need a new car.* But out of respect I didn't want to be a nagging child, but the little things kept becoming more obvious. It wouldn't be right to turn a blind eye and pretend they didn't mean anything. This went on for a few weeks.

I was at the bank one day, and the manager, who I know, gives me a hug. I dropped the keys and the clicker (remote opener) breaks all apart. This was the final bit in a pattern of seeming coincidences. I got back in my car and I said, *Lord I get it! We need a new car.*

I suggested to my friend, "Maybe one day we can go to the place I got my Mitsubishi and look at cars for the fun of it. Two weeks later she was having a problem and called. "I need to get away. Do you want to look at cars?" I was on my way to the gym, but I knew this was another step in getting a new car, so I took a break from my daily routine and said, "Let's go."

We get to the dealership and of course the salespeople are all around me, even the manager came out. I told them all that I'm not really interested so they wouldn't nag me. I said, "The only car I would consider is a red convertible." The manager said (to my relief) we don't have any, so the pressure was off.

Well, the salesman came over, who is also from Venezuela, and we were talking away having a good time. And then he says, "Come with me, I want to show you something."

I'm thinking, *Okay why not.* Lo and behold, he brings me to a beautiful red convertible that is exactly what I wanted! I ask, "How come this is here when the manager said there are none on the lot?"

He explained, "The owner of this car has been here three times to buy a car, but he did not want to trade this in. But the third time, he suddenly changed his mind and here it is. You're the first person to see it."

Then I saw how all these little things added up. God was leading me to buy this car; how could I refuse? After all, I am his daughter and he wants me to be happy. So I offered to put money down and they said we trust you, no deposit needed. Again things were working out according to a pattern.

There comes a time when you recognize things are happening in a way that's not mere chance. You're being guided from above. When that happens you become a channel for a higher energy—knowingness—to enter. And that is how we should live, always connected to the energy source. Learn how to connect to the Divine Presence within and stay that way; make it your first order of business. It is how life is designed and it becomes so much easier when we cooperate.

LONG-TERM
RELATIONSHIPS

Likes attract and unlikes separate

There are minds that flow in remarkably similar channels. There is a term for this, "kindred minds." This is one reason people are attracted to one other. So it makes sense that people are more likely to be in agreement and cooperate when their minds are alike.

By contrast, with dissimilar minds you can share only so deeply and unify only so much. Don't be fooled that it is enough for both of you to like being outdoors, fishing and hiking. These are outward tastes and are not enough for the long haul. It is why you need a long enough time of courtship so you really get to know one another. But variety in taste doesn't always mean your minds are dissimilar. A man likes hunting and a woman enjoys cooking. They can still be like-minded and have similar spiritual natures (kindred spirits).

Kindred minds have philosophies of personal living that are in tune with the master philosophy of the universe. Such people have a rich interior life, one in which they reflect upon the issues of living:

- the highest sense of right and wrong (moral duty),
- the utmost truth of the situation,
- the greatest good for the most people, and
- the most beautiful outcome they can imagine.

It is by such reflective thinking that decisions are no longer driven by a person's animal nature, by what other people think, and by what the culture says is right. No. You now make choices based on your higher mind, philosophy of living, spiritual insight, and divine guidance.

For two individuals, several people, or a working group to be truly unified, they must believe in something higher than themselves. The highest possible belief is the source of all Reality—God. It is why the United States was founded on *One Nation under God*. This commonality of belief is what unites all its citizens regardless of how diverse their backgrounds. So it is with individuals. The degree of harmony is determined by their shared belief in something higher than themselves. Some degree of shared morals and spiritual agreement is essential to friendship between two persons.

Unity is not subscribing to the same doctrines and religious rituals. Rather, it's sharing the same aspiration to find the Father of all and be instructed by him. This quest is what unites not only two people in intimate union but also people everywhere. This is why spirit-led people recognize one another.

Unfortunately, there is a retrogression going on in which it has become fashionable among so-called sophisticated people to look down on those with faith in God as wishful thinking, fantasy, or delusion. They seek to substitute the god of mind. People may be like-minded, but unless they subject their will to that of God, relationships will deteriorate, disintegrate, and end in bitterness and fighting.

An example of like-mindedness

My writing coach and I were trying to decide on a picture for the cover of this book. Because the topic is about relationships it seemed reasonable to have me with one or several people on the cover. And we selected a picture of myself and a friend having a good time.

The selection of this picture is rational, but is it right? Is it the truth for this cover?

Several days after we decided on this picture, it wasn't feeling right to me and I thought it best to continue what we did with the other books and have a picture of me only. So I sent an email to

Coach saying so at 6:05 AM. I receive an email from him at 6:06 AM saying the same thing, but he had not received my email yet! Now that's an example of two things: 1) we think alike; 2) we were both in touch with our feelings; it didn't sit right which prompted us to think about it some more, and we each came up with the same conclusion. A thrilling confirmation of the right decision!

Marriage and self-respect

A successful intimate relationship (actually, all relationships) requires a sense of responsibility to who you are. Your relationship is in grave danger if you do not respect yourself enough to be true to what you think and how you feel—your true identity. For example, I hope you will love me more if I eat what you eat, think what you think, and do what you do. It's the opposite. Love is about you being you and me being me.

There's too much manipulation in relationships. People think it gives them the right to control you if they provide things you need. That's not love, that's slavery. You think that because you go to work and bring in the money that you can treat me however you want. You don't love me when you see me as something you can use, thinking all I'm doing is staying home and keeping your clothes clean and making a nice place to live. That's not love. And neither is it love when you give from duty.

There are relationships in which one person is always giving, giving, giving, and the other one is just taking, taking, taking. The person giving doesn't realize that the relationship isn't working. If I continue giving because I have a need to be loved, I am lying to myself, saying "Because I give you things we will have a good relationship." It doesn't work like that. Find out who you are. What is it that you like and don't like? And then be courageous enough to be real—even though there might be consequences. But it's wise to count the cost so you know what to expect and prepare for the possibility.

I address what follows to the ladies because throughout our history the culture has been male-dominated. See yourself as daughters of God in your own right. Recognize your own strength and your own value. Your foundation in life does not depend on your spouse, your children, your parents, your career, or whatever role you find yourself in. It depends upon your commitment to be perfect as God is perfect, and thereby be whole in yourself.

Marriage and different tastes

A woman told me this story. "I have to stop eating like my husband eats. He likes popcorn but that doesn't work for me." I said to her, "It is okay for him to have popcorn. But you don't have to eat his popcorn if you want a banana with peanut butter. The point is you are sharing the pleasure of eating together."

This is where self-respect comes in. You know yourself well enough to say, *What do I want to eat as we share time together?* Without having confidence in who you are, you will go along with what he likes to please him and end up damaging yourself. This is not uncommon. A couple gets married and both are thin. The husband usually doesn't put on much weight but his wife blows up. Why? Because she starts eating as her husband eats. He can have three hamburgers and he is skinny as could be. You take a bite and you gain five pounds!

When I was dating my husband he was a big breakfast eater. So I ate what he did, which included lots of bread with peanut butter and other spreads. Of course it wasn't long before I gained 20 pounds. Yikes! You can imagine that I learned from that experience to eat how I need to. Good lesson to be true to myself.

So how do two people deal with different tastes and what works in their bodies without feeling you've done something wrong? Love does not want your partner to feel guilty for being himself or herself. A loving relationship requires respect for each another's choices. It's absurd to think that because I'm married to you I can't go to the gym. No! it doesn't work that way.

A wholesome relationship requires sharing ideas and activities. The guy likes to go hunting and to football games and his wife doesn't care for them. Let him go. On the other hand she likes to go shopping, so he must respect that and let her have a good time. Two people will always have different tastes; you can't like all the same things.

You have to compromise if you want a happy relationship. For example, a wife doesn't want to feel like a football widow; the game is always more important than she is. And her husband doesn't want to feel like his wife is a shopaholic and shopping is more important than he is. Here's an example of a compromise: I'll go to the game with you sometimes because you love it and want to share it with me, and you come shopping with me because you love me and I want to share what I love with you.

When is it time to separate?

There is a time in a relationship when separation may be the healthiest thing you can do. Why is this? Because neither of you can grow. It's like a shoe that's too small; you feel cramped; it no longer fits you. We falsely believe that for the rest of our lives we must stay in the role of a father or mother, husband or wife, grandparent, whatever. You don't have to be stuck in one role forever if you need to make a change so you can grow.

Now, if you have a loving partner, they are going to encourage you to follow your heart, even though your new direction may upset things. Each should support the other as a maturing personality. If you need to go your own way to some degree, then separation to that degree is healthy. If you want to fly, your loved one should encourage you to spread your wings. Love lets live and encourages you to become all you can be.

Divorce

Hopefully, a person who is changing her path is supported by her husband, or a wife encourages her husband to pursue his vision. That's best of course. But there are times when stubbornness and refusal to give up power and authority make it impossible to follow your dream if you remain together. That's when divorce makes sense. This can be legal if you're married, or permanent separation if you are living together, or in spirit if it works better to stay together in the same house. It takes wise judgment to determine the solution when you have grown apart. But always let love, wisdom, and kindness overshadow what you decide. Seek the best for the other without sacrificing what God shows you to do.

Here is a story of God answering a question from a woman about divorcing her husband.[1]

---

[1] Rosen, Richard. (2016). DEAR ABBA: God answers heartfelt questions of everyday living. p.40.

Dear Abba,

My husband and I have been married 12 years and we have two children. We are both miserable. How do you look upon divorce?

Ready to Divorce

Dear Ready to Divorce,

I do not like divorce. Nevertheless, it is not a sacred duty to remain together. Marriage is a human institution only for this life. It does not continue into the next.

Marriage is about relationship. The purpose of two people intimately sharing their lives is to assist each other become spiritual and well-rounded. Men and women are inherently different. Marriage, therefore, is like sandpaper wearing away irritations, thereby overcoming them. It is a wonderful learning and maturing for those willing to be smoothed out.

Be mindful that issues within yourself that you fail to resolve during this marriage will follow you into future relationships. So do not fool yourself into thinking it is an escape. It is not.

It is crucial that you be honest, be genuine, and be sincere with yourself. Consult with me. Ask me to show you if you could have done better, if you participated in making things difficult. Let it not be said that you contributed to the dissolution of this partnership.

Nonetheless, if you have reached the place where you can no longer withstand being together, I understand that. But it is preferable, especially with children, to remain together and work it out. However, assuming you and your husband have genuinely made the effort, together and with outside resources, and have concluded it is not possible, then divorce would be best. Then each of you can begin life anew, either singly or with someone who will help you become all you are capable of becoming.

Romantic Love

I want to be clear that no matter how intense your feelings are for someone, your most important relationship is with God and his will for you, and being true to yourself—integrity. No one comes before that no matter how you feel about them. It must be worked on diligently and daily until it becomes your life. You can look at it as serving God in others and serving God in yourself. Both are necessary.

From this eternal source of love emanates the intense feelings of romance. But don't set yourself up for disappointment. Studies show that romantic love lasts two years, during which the brain is bathed in happy hormones. Then it returns to normal and romance ideally transforms into loving friendship deepened amidst the routines and necessities of daily living.

We need to be realistic and realize that intensely romantic relationships (and relationships in general) reflect an energy that's always changing. I have a friend who got divorced. A few years later she remarried. Guess what? She's getting divorced again! I remember their happy faces during the wedding, their vows and promises of eternal love. What happened? Things change. Being aware of a new trend in a relationship enables you to adapt while remaining true to yourself.

I have found that anyone may disappoint you, but God never lets you down. When you made it your business to know yourself, then disappointment becomes a learning experience. No matter how awful the situation you will never disappoint yourself. This means that you stand strong in your core values and remain faithful to your inner voice.

People close to you may feel threatened as you evolve physically, mentally, and spiritually. They subconsciously don't want you to change. Be careful; don't give in and give up on yourself to please others; don't do it!

This is why I strongly believe in loving God with all your heart and mind and loving yourself (self-respect). From this foundation you will be clear about who you are and what a beautiful romantic relationship you have with the best lover ever—God!

FAMILY

Families you come from

My brother Edmundo

Family is the cornerstone of relationships. It's where you learn how to be with others. But the family you come from can be complicated because you had no choice in the matter. Depending on your experience, it either prepares you for loving relationships or sets you up for failure—at least until you take control and undo the bad influences.

Nonetheless, your birth family entails moral duty, as the commandment says, "Honor your father and mother." They are your source, your roots, and will always be your family. You have an obligation to respect, help, and do whatever good you can.

Furthermore, there is a bond—a deep one—with your mother and father and brothers and sisters. These are the people you grew up with and shared so many experiences. It is unique and you can never know others in the same way. Even after loved ones have died they remain alive in the next world. That's why you hear someone say, "I feel their spirit." And when you leave this world, what a grand reunion it is when you all meet, hug, and share your stories. You will tell them what's been happening on earth, and they will fill you in on what to expect in the next stage of your life.

A note of caution: There are family relationships that have deteriorated, sometimes becoming dangerous, even toxic. In this case, it is wise to separate from your family for your protection and self-preservation.

Families you create

The family you create is by choice: who you marry and the children you have.

Over the years your children see the evidence of how you raised them which stay with them. For example, I had affirmations all over the house. Their friends would read them, and being teenagers, would become embarrassed about all this positive thinking. It seemed strange, and it certainly didn't happen in their homes. Who is this weird mom? Now that my children are adults, they do the same thing; they post affirmations throughout their homes. The rituals I created stayed with my children. And they have in turn created their own rituals. For example, my daughter Arianna calls going to the gym her ritual.

I am the example to my children of how to live, demonstrated by things like the affirmations I posted. But more importantly, it's because I am real with them. They know I don't have hidden motives when we talk. As a result, they feel that I do things from love and not duty; my authenticity comes from a higher place. When you come from a relationship with God, you become more kind and loving with your family. How I live and my words therefore stay with my children and mold their lives. As it is written, "Train up a child in the way he should go, and when he is old he will not depart from it" (Proverbs 22:6).

Children

Parenthood is a serious business. I had my children in my mid-thirties. I had a great job and I was making good money. It was right for me to have children; I could provide for them.

That's one of the many responsibilities of being a parent—provide a good home for your children, be a loving mother or father, meet all their basic needs such as food and doctors.

I had my children and no longer mother them, telling them, "Do this and do that." When I was at the stage of being a mom, I did it 100%. That's why I don't worry about my kids now. They have made their own relationships with God and reality. Even if it's negative, that's what's needed for them to grow, to gain the experience of what works and what doesn't.

Now we visit, go shopping, and do things together. No longer is it my role to direct their lives. I raised them the best I could to be loving, responsible adults; now they must chart their own way. I'm not going to be a mother at 72 and tell my children how to live. That's not my role. Let live, let be. That's love.

While raising my children it wasn't so much that they learned from what I said, but what they saw me do, what I modeled. You can't fool children with words that differ from your behavior; they have an intuitive sense; they know. You teach children by how you live more than by what you say. You model your behavior, you model your faith, you model how you achieve things, how you got your car, how you got a house. They see and learn; that's the best way to bring up a child. Show more, tell less.

Once you fulfill your duties the best you can, and things go south, don't worry because you know how you raised them. And certainly don't beat yourself up. Many parents feel guilty because their children choose a destructive path. That's their choice; it's their lives. You did the best you could. You provided a good home, good opportunities, and were a good role model. You didn't do drugs or alcohol; you didn't smoke. They could have learned from you, but they chose a harmful way. So be it! You still love them and you respect their choice. As the saying goes, you hate the sin but love the sinner.

But what if you were a poor role model and lived with destructive habits? Again, don't beat yourself up. Remember that God lives within them and can help them overcome any negativity if they are willing. There are so many stories of people who came out of awful situations and became fine human beings. You made your mistakes, told God you are sorry for them and changed. What more can you do? So just live and refuse to feel guilty for what God has already forgiven.

Always choose the healthy path for yourself regardless of what your children do with their lives. Remember, *you* are the most important person in the world. Do your best. That's what I did with my daughters. I don't worry about them. I am not the type of mom who's constantly wondering or worried. I know who I raised. Let your children live their lives; they'll appreciate your confidence in them and love you for it.

Danielle and Adriana

Adriana wrote to me, "The only lasting relationship is the one you have with God." It made me feel good, that I did the best I could as a mom.

RELATIONSHIP BEYOND FAMILY

Strangers

What is your attitude as you go about your chores and activities? When you go to the bank and the grocery store, how do you talk to the people you meet there? Are you shining a light or pouring out darkness, cursing and upset, blaming everyone, and being nasty?

Why is it important how I am with the attendant at the coffee shop? Why must I care about them? Why should I be nice to the helper who asks, "How can I help you?"

Acquaintances have the same degree of importance as long-term relationships. In my world it means a lot to be kind to everyone who's providing you a service. What happens when you care about the bank teller, the cashier at the grocery store, the attendant at the car wash, the receptionist at your gym, your mechanic, the staff at your doctor's office? You will be delighted with the quality of service you receive. It's because you always—and I mean always—have an uplifting attitude towards them. It also has a material benefit as Earl Nightingale spoke about: every dollar you make is based on successful relationships with others.

Being kind to strangers comes back to your relationship with God. You love them because you love God. God not only loves you but also loves them. His Spirit indwells them as he does you. They have a guardian angel as you do.

Try this exercise to help you become more loving to *everyone* you meet. Think of each person as a brother or sister you did not know, children of the same heavenly Father. Look for the unique portion of the divine personality given to them. After death you may meet that clerk who asked if she could help you. How are you going to feel then if you are nasty now? See yourself meeting them in the next life and talking over when you were together, even if it's only this one time. Don't you want to have a good memory? How did I treat them? Did I care about them? Did they feel it?

Here's an example of how I saw things in a higher way in order to encourage and empower a young man filled with fear.

I went to the beauty school to have my roots retouched. I always ask for a student who is experienced, someone ready to graduate. However, this time I didn't. Instead I followed the flow. I noticed a student who seemed timid and kind of lost. And that's the kid who the instructor assigned to do my hair! I thought, *Oh no, he looks so insecure!*

I was going to place my purse on the counter of his station, but it was full of trimmings. I thought no way I would put my belongings on that hairy counter. Not a good beginning.

I gave him the product I use and clearly said, "Only the roots, not my highlights." You can tell I wasn't confident of the outcome. He looked at me surprised and repeated what I said, and I confirmed, "Yes, only the roots." Off he goes to ask the instructor what to do. OMG, I was ready to walk out!

The instructor came over and I told her I was concerned because he looked so insecure and scared. The instructor nonverbally agreed with me. I asked if she could assign someone else. Then she herself began applying the color and told him to watch how it is done.

We were talking and I told the instructor that I was doing homework for my writing coach for my third book. She got all excited. I told her about my first book and offered it for doing my hair. I then asked Clinton, the

35

student, if he would like one. He gave me a big smile and said, Yes!

At that moment the instructor and I were drawn into Clinton's need and felt inspired. We explained how important it is to radiate confidence when you approach your clients. I suggested to Clinton that my books and YouTube channel, <u>DrJosefina</u>[2], are resources that can help him. It was an anointed moment.

I gave them both my book. Clinton was happy, smiling, and feeling better about himself, so much so that he said that he would post the experience on Facebook.

What began as anxiety about my hair ended with the empowerment of a young life. Relationships can be for a few minutes, hours, or years. It doesn't matter; we are always impacting people.

I enjoy so much meeting people. Getting to know someone is fascinating because there is a kaleidoscope of experiences that make each person unique; you will never meet another like them. It's an adventure. So if you're bored, become interested in others, seek to understand their problems and joys; that's how you come to love them. (But this doesn't mean you're a busybody.)

Everyone can use a lift. It touches their soul to feel that you care, that you appreciate who they are and see the good in them. The moment you are nice to someone you lighten their day and bring a smile to their face. They were having a lousy day but feel better because of your good energy.

God is always using us as a vehicle of his love, kindness, joy, and hope. People will see you and say, *She has something special.* And what is it they see? It comes from your relationship with the Divine; that's what they see living through you. People want hope and you can give it to them. Hope is a good friend who keeps you alive and smiling.

Good relationships follow when you consecrate to being a vessel of light. You are guided to the right person and led to say the right thing because you are love saturated.

---

[2] My YouTube channel: https://www.youtube.com/user/drjosefina/playlists

Groups

Good relationships allow people to work together in harmony. A measure of intellectual keenness and emotional maturity is being aware of how everyone is connected. Your well-being depends on the well-being of everyone else.

As you develop your skill at communicating, you will stimulate one another's minds to think new thoughts and undertake new possibilities. By associating with loving, understanding, and compassionate people, you will escape the conditioning of how you were raised and your current situation. You will expand your range of living. What's more, it's a delight to get to know others.

Most people are unaware of how influenced they are by others. There is a different energy package each time you are with people. Each person in a gathering affects every other. The group dynamic changes whenever someone comes or leaves.

Each individual has strengths and weaknesses. Love seeks to understand the strengths and have compassion for the weaknesses. Love treats everyone fairly. This allows gatherings, associations, committees, and groups to work together at their highest level and achieve the best results.

HANDFULS OF PURPOSE

Self-respect

How can I not feel good about myself when God created me and he did so perfectly! Am I going to tell him he made a mistake? Know that God made you perfect, just as you should be (not the junk we inherit and pick up along the way). He gave you a portion of his personality for you to express. It's our job (and it's an adventure) to discover who we are purposed to be. This is how we become authentic, genuine, and sincere.

So many people do not have a relationship with God—at least not an everyday one. Why is this? Three reasons:

1. We inherit negative inclinations from our parents, grandparents, and ancestors. It's in the genes (but there are also good things we get).
2. We are brought up in harmful and unwholesome environments.
3. We make poor choices and reject the values of eternity for the short-term pleasures of self-gratification.

As a result there is subconscious voice and feeling that makes you feel like you've done something wrong, that you are not a good person. You don't feel good about yourself—and guilt is a poor mate in a relationship.

People think to themselves, *I'm so embarrassed; I really messed my life up.* Okay, what's new! You're in good company. So what do you do now? Think of the most loving human parent you can and know that God loves you way more than that. He knows *everything* about you and he cares about you just the same. He knows you want to and will get better. It's when you recognize his confidence in you that you can forgive and learn to love yourself as he does. This is self-respect.

To begin with, be sure to focus on what's right with you and not what's wrong. Here are some additional ideas.

There are…ways for you to show yourself some love.[3]
On a daily basis, ask yourself the question, "If I truly loved

---

[3] Wentz, Isabella. (2017). Hashimoto's Protocol: A 90-Day Plan for Reversing Thyroid Symptoms and Getting Your Life Back. HarperOne. p.295.

myself, what would I do?" If you're looking for suggestions, here is a list of some acts of self-compassion:

- Take a hot bath with no time limit.
- Get a massage.
- Buy yourself a special treat.
- Nourish yourself with great food.
- Say kind words to yourself.
- Speak your truth.
- Take a nap.
- Do something really nice for yourself.
- Ask for help when you need it.
- Talk to someone who will listen and not judge.

Once you feel good about yourself, then you can feel good about others, respect them, and love them. You cannot respect yourself more than you love others, and you cannot love others more than you respect yourself. How loyal to love are you? You will know by the degree it governs your life, values such as kindness, mercy, and compassion. I would add, *listen and not judge*, all too often missing in the world.

People have limitations; recognize and accept them; it's the way it is. They also have strengths. But in either case do not blindly follow how they live. Let them live as they want; love lets live. Don't think they need your advice. Allow people to make their own decisions, whether you think them good or bad. You are not God; they have God living within them who knows better than you what they need and what they are able to receive.

Work on yourself

For me to have good relationships I must keep transforming myself. The process of transformation gets me to the place where my heart is aligned with my spirit. As a result, I am vibrant whatever my age. I know where I have been, I know where I am now, and I know where I am going.

As more light comes into me, the more I share it with others. I am an empty vessel through whom the Divine Source of light and love proceeds. I refuse to be selfish and hog it for myself. I let love out to do its thing. That is a choice each of us must make.

So I work on myself to become the person God has destined. How do I do that? I pursue the divine will with all my strength. Here's how you know what that will is: for each decision you make determine what is:

- the highest truth of the matter (what's really going on);
- the greatest good that will benefit the most people; and
- the most beautiful outcome you can imagine.

How well do you know yourself? You can't know someone else if you do not know who you are. What part of you is from above? What values do you cherish that are from eternity? From this comes believing in yourself and trusting in the potential of others.

Your life is predestined to go a certain way. You can discover your life pattern if you study it. But it's up to you to get in the car and go along for the ride. It may not be a Rolls-Royce, but you'll have something that runs well, even though it's a plain old Chevy.

It's what you need at this time in your life; otherwise you would have something else. Are you driving on the road prepared for you? Or would you rather go your own way, choosing self-will over the divine will? That some choice, isn't it? I'm being frank because I don't want you to miss out being the person you are meant to be. I want you to be vibrant.

You become a new person when you know who you are. You see things differently, from a higher perspective, through the eyes of love and compassion. Good energy goes before you wherever you go. You vibrate at a high frequency when you enter a room. People cannot help but notice. And depending on what's in them, they will be either attracted or repelled by you. But don't worry; you're just being you; everything will fall into place. Isn't this a worthwhile goal? Isn't it worth your time and energy? I think so and that's why I have pursued the divine plan of my life with gusto. And you can do the same.

It takes effort

It sounds good to have loving relationships where people work well together and live in harmony, but it does not come without dedication. It takes effort to build relationships. And many people would rather take it easy. They innately know that they will encounter struggle and conflict as they learn to work things out and resolve differences. Conflict arises when you are set in your ways, refusing to change "preconceived opinions, settled ideas, and long-standing prejudices."

What if you met this woman? Would you be able to relate to her?

Will you stay in your comfortable and settled ways? Or will you move out of your comfort zone and look for the good in people and show yourself friendly?

Once you've consecrated your will to loving relationships, and have done the work to make them happen, you will enter into the delight of having caring people in your life. Healthy relationships become normal and no longer require the effort they once did. You make the most of being together. You take delight in cultivating relationships to everyone's benefit.

Intuition and relationships

Cease trying to work everything out with your minds, it will get you nowhere. Live by intuition and inspiration and let your whole life be a Revelation. (Eileen Caddy)

True relationships are not haphazard. The seeming coincidence of meeting someone who changes our lives is not accidental. No! It is arranged according to Gods plan provided we cooperate. God has his divine plan and we have our human one. It's our decision whether or not to choose God's plan; that's what free will is about. It's when you choose to align yourself with the career God has prepared for you that things work out.

The way I use my intuition is by listening or feeling the promptings of the Spirit. You can also think of it as your indwelling God fragment. Sometimes I feel a sensation in my body, a peculiar tingling, and I know it's the Spirit. It often happens when I am resting in bed. It's sweet, peaceful, and empowering. That's what Jesus meant when he promised to send the Holy Spirit who will teach you all things.

The Spirit arranges relationships for our growth. You just need to sense his subtle guidance. This is how intuition makes a way for you. The purpose may be a beautiful friendship of shared lives. Or people may be brought together for a project. When seen in this light, do not the apparent ordinary events of living become a challenge and adventure? Does not life become more meaningful as you recognize there's a reason for what happens?

Here are some ways you recognize intuition:

sixth sense	gut feeling	impression
knowingness	thought	nudge
mind picture	insight	perception

Intuition will spare you from difficult and dangerous situations. The Spirit Within knows what's coming and what you need to do for the best possible outcome. He gives you insight into people and situations, guiding you into them or away from them.

Recognize that intuition is a valuable resource for your good. Strive to develop it; exercise it; it doesn't come without effort. Trusting your intuition will improve your relationships immensely; it will serve you well.

The following message is from the perspective of a celestial personality (edited).

If you do not hear words as messages, perhaps you can feel us energetically and kinesthetically. Perhaps you notice those guiding intuitions that bring about synchronicities that benefit your spiritual growth and contact with others. Perhaps you will perceive they are not fantastic coincidences but arranged events.

We bend and twist in every possible way to bring you into the most beneficial contacts and opportunities for your spiritual growth and spiritual education, for your soul development. We neglect you not! No one is neglected, from the most humble and seemingly destitute to the wealthiest, most selfish, and seemingly unworthy. We reach out every moment to enfold you in loving embrace and bring you to the higher purpose, with all your life events and all your seeming challenges.[4]

Ultimately it is through a union of mind and spirit that we are guided. You can grow only so much relying on mind alone. If you depend mostly on your analytical mind and distrust your heart, only half of you is present in a relationship. You unknowingly are holding back a part of yourself. Learn to trust your heart. As it is written, "A good man out of the good treasure of the heart brings forth good things" (Matthew 12:35).

---

[4] Nebadonia. Spiritual Fruits, Guiding Intuition. (10.07.2006). Daynal Institute. http://nordan.daynal.org/wiki/index.php?title=2006-10-07-Spiritual_Fruits,_Guiding_Intuition

How my intuition led me to Cartagena

This is where I ended up because I followed my spirit.
Life's an adventure!

(Note: I'm telling you in detail what I did during this trip to give you an idea of how I live my life and what my days are like.)

A few months ago Adriana, my daughter, went to Cartagena, Colombia to attend a friend's wedding. She posted some pictures of this beautiful city and instantly I felt a very strong impression to go there. I couldn't get it out of my mind. I didn't know why I should visit (which I learned after I got there). I thought after a few days it would go away, but several weeks went by and that voice would remind me, *You have to go to Cartagena.*

Sometimes we look for reasons not to obey, things like money. It just so happened that I had credit for a plane ticket from a trip to New York I had canceled. Ok, now money is not an excuse.

One morning during my Ritual the Voice once again said, *We are going to Cartagena*. Finally I agreed. I decided on a date, came home, and booked the flight. From that time on I felt myself in a wonderful place.

My daughter Danielle suggested that I drive to her house and she would drop me off at the airport. How can I refuse an offer to share time with those I love? I got to her place; she took me out for lunch; we went shopping; we had a great time.

Everything was going well and it continued when I suggested it might be better to Uber to the airport; she said no problem. The driver of the Uber car and I got along beautifully. He starting talking about wellness and got so excited when I told him that's my area of expertise. He will get my books for himself and his wife. He felt the energy as we laughed and had a blast. He said, "Josefina, you made my day. I will end work early." We exchanged information, hugged, and said our goodbyes. That's what it's like to connect in spirit as you go through the day.

All these things confirmed my leading to go to Cartagena, which my intuition kept confirming, and which I trusted.

Things continued in the same vein at the airport. As I was going through security I did a double biceps and the security people imitated me and we all laughed. I went to get a snack, a banana, and not only did the lady not charge me, I discovered later that she put in three bananas instead of one! Another delightful confirmation of following what God had shown me. And things continued like this when the airline as a courtesy didn't charge me for my bag and gave me an excellent seat.

Why was I treated that way? Because I was caring and friendly, like remembering and saying their names. I listened to the banana lady tell me about her son doing drugs. I always find something good about them and say so. I'm interested in and care about people; they feel and respond to it. Be mindful to thank others and show appreciation. It makes them feel good about themselves. Because it brings out their best they want to be helpful.

My flight took off on time and I was in Cartagena by 3 PM. I walked outside looking for a sign with my name and there was none. (So here's a little drama. I'll see where it goes and not get freaked out.) I asked about a shuttle to the Conrad Hotel and the gentlemen said, "There is none, you need to take a taxi"; he points me to a driver and I said okay. I got in the taxi with Eric and his business partner Oscar. By the time we arrived at the hotel we agreed that they would take care of my transportation while in Cartagena. They said, "Everything will be relaxed, no rushing. We are here to serve and also protect you." That made me feel good.

See how it worked out that the person who was to meet me at the airport wasn't there. That allowed me to meet these two fine gentlemen. Another confirmation of God leading me while I do my part to cooperate.

As soon as we stopped at the hotel, a young man opened the door and escorted me to the registration desk. There a beautiful woman name Angelica, with an angel face, took care of my reservation. A young man came with a tray and a hot towel for me to refresh. A few seconds later another young fellow came with a tray and a glass of fresh juice. When I saw all this I said to them, "Wait a minute! We need to video this!" And that's when the ice broke and formality went out the window. We were all laughing as we posed for pictures and videos. We had fun and everyone one was saying POW!

From that moment they went out of their way to make sure I was comfortable and had everything I needed.

After checking into my beautiful suite I walked around the grounds, delighting in the beauty. I was surrounded by birds chirping, the smell of the flowers, a peace and serenity that connects you effortlessly with your inner self. Now I was the one saying POW!

I checked the gym and spa, everything first class. For dinner one of the assistants suggested *camarones al ajillo*. OMG, it was divine, and a fresh salad.

My daughter Adriana had posted pictures of herself at the beach in Miami where there were people, umbrellas, beach chairs, and lots of action.

But looking from my room in Cartagena I thought, oh my God, where are the people? It made me feel lonely, that I wanted to be with my daughter in Miami. I began questioning God's plan; did I make a mistake? Following your inner guidance is not banana peel easy. But the more you do it, the more confident you become and the better you get at it, like exercising a muscle. The formula is simple: believe God, follow his instructions, and he does the rest.

It wasn't until the next day that I learned the reason why I was in Cartagena, which I'll tell you later. Meanwhile, Eric and Oscar, my guides, took me to some wonderful places. We visited la Iglesia de Santo Domingo, beautiful. The three of us knelt and prayed.

For lunch they took me to Bony, a famous restaurant owned by a former Olympic boxer. They fish from the ocean and cook it right there. Sitting there I thanked God for the peace of the hotel because it didn't let in the vendors who are always after you to buy their merchandise. I know it means food on the table for their families, but enough is enough. False sentimentality doesn't help others or make for good decisions.

Eric and Oscar showed me how they were protecting and watching after me. At the beginning of our tour I asked about getting coffee. Of course, they said no problem. We stopped at a market with fruits, and I am crazy about fruit! I paid, was distracted, and walked out without the fruit; but Oscar was paying attention and took them. Another time I dropped my bag on the street to dance with one of the beautiful women who carry trays of food on their heads and can still dance cumbia. My protectors were alert and picked up my bag right away.

When we got back in the car I thanked them for being watchful. They replied, "We are here to serve and protect you." It made me feel good.

Saturday I had an awesome workout with Francisco, one of the trainers at the hotel. After I finished the delicious steam room, they showed me a locker where I found everything I needed, including a nice white bikini, lol. I was at least three hours on my workout and in the spa. When I was lying down doing yoga I had a déjà vu; I had been here before. Then I saw myself doing retreats here; it was the perfect place.

My inner voice said *Talk to the manager*, so I asked to see her. Turns out we met at check-in so we already knew each other. I told her about my idea of a retreat and that many people follow me. Immediately she said, "I know, my husband is one of them!" Wow! "I know all about you because he follows your morning Ritual." OMG, incredible! She was on board without me saying more. And things got even better. She said, "It just so happens that my boss is here today for a meeting and I will present your idea." She continued, "In June there is a global day of wellness and the hotel is interested in participating, so this fits right in." I told her I am available then to do a retreat. Now I knew why I came to Cartagena.

By 11 AM Eric came to pick me up and take me to a lovely beach. He insisted that I should go there. It's called Baru, about 50 minutes from Cartagena. I said, "It makes me feel happy; let's go!" You can see videos of Baru on my YouTube channel.

Eric told me that when we get to Baru people will offer to show you around, but stay with me. My friends Manuel and Willy will take care of you.

José Carlos, Willie, Eric, and Manuel

We went to Manuel's aunt, who cooked steamed fish (they go to the ocean and fish for lunch) with salad and fried green plantains (*tostones*), another delicious dish, POW!

Baru is an island and everything has to be brought in. Life is hard for them but they are happy. Manuel and Willie were excellent guides and we had a terrific day. I gave them a good tip; they were worthy. As we were leaving, Manuel put his hand on my shoulder and said, "I need to tell you something. Because of you my mother, wife, and daughter will eat today." OMG! I said to him, "Manuel give thanks to God." Isn't that what life is all about?

Finally my trip came to an end. On the way back to the airport Eric thanked me profusely for my business and for being down to earth and humble. You brought a blessing to my family, my wife, and my two children." That touched me.

I don't know if you have been to a place that you don't want to leave; you want to return because of the relationships. It's people who make the difference, not things or places. Everyone wants to be treated with respect and feel their lives matter, that they are important whatever they do or however they live.

* * *

What does this long story have to do with relationships? Because I was sensitive to my indwelling fragment of God leading me, I met new people and we added something to one another's lives that makes us better human beings. If you want to better hear your Spirit, the best way is wholehearted and loving service to your brothers and sisters. This is how you exercise spiritually.

Share your life

I'm going to say something that may sound strange to you. It is not so important to end up with a good relationship as how you go about it. For example, you cannot use deceit to trap a husband, even though you may bag him. Not a good beginning! You can't create a good relationship by wanting it badly. It doesn't work that way because you end up cutting corners (and you may not even know it because you're desperate). You need to do things right. If you're meant to be together, it will happen by being your loving, authentic self. Wholesome relationships come from a heartfelt concern for the welfare of others and helping them become the best they can be. Someone will love you when they feel you care about them. Simple, isn't it?

You must share your life if you want good relationships. People would love you for the many good things in your life if they knew this part of you. Your sharing nourishes their love and respect.

Do you want others to trust you? You earn their trust first by living a life of honesty and integrity with yourself. Then by your actions people learn that you keep your word and they can trust you.

Something of great value emerges from friendships based on mutual respect, forgiveness, patience, and tolerance. Each comes away changed. Each allows the energy of their hearts to flow into the other. Each shares their creativity and makes the other more than they were.

A word of caution: Relationships can be like a fruit salad or a smoothie. In a fruit salad each fruit keeps its unique flavor, color, and taste—its integrity. You remain the unique individual that you are. By contrast, in a smoothie each fruit gets lost in the mix; you lose your identity, purpose, and uniqueness in the name of so-called love. It's not. Don't homogenize who you are to avoid making waves for the sake of harmony.

Here is a guaranteed way to improve your relationships. With intention exercise the fruits of the spirit with everyone you meet. These are some of the fruits (there are others that you can add to your own list). Think about each one carefully. How much is in your life? If you asked others who know you well, would they agree?

Love	Kindness
Joy	Tolerance
Peace	Long-suffering
Mercy	Unfailing forgiveness

Think of each spiritual value as a muscle. The more you exercise them the more they improve your relationship with others. They give you control. You are no longer a sailboat subject to the slightest emotional breeze; you are now the captain of the (relation)ship.

Draw out your soul to strangers. Which of the fruits do they need? Which ones would they appreciate? Do good for the simple reason that you love people and want to see them better off. You do not need to know the effect you have on their lives, but there will be one. And it will spread as they share the goodness in their lives.

Embrace the small kindnesses of living. Despise not the day of small things for they are by which your soul grows. Be alert to offer an encouraging word to a stressed cashier, a smile to a passerby, a warm greeting to a neighbor, a helping hand to someone struggling with a door, an invitation to enter a traffic lane. People will respond. When you hug someone, don't they hug you back? And so you have a two-way energy flow. As you give of yourself, your soul opens as a flower to receive more divine energy and you become fragrant. The aroma of friendliness prepares the way for enduring closeness.

Sincere communication

To be successful in your relationships you must truly hear one another. Carefully listen to all the ways someone is talking to you: strong feelings, body language, words of course, and thoughts that you discern, a kind of telepathy. Take time to hear—what are they really saying? What does their heart tell you?

This is where your intuition pays off. Sometimes it's good to repeat in your own words what someone is saying; you want to be sure you got it right. And it lets them know you care enough to really listen.

Be sure there are no hidden motives, some you may not even be aware of, that color your relationships. Your intuition will help you here; you must know yourself. Have it as a goal to be love saturated. Then people are more likely to drop their doubts, suspicions, and defenses and be loving in return.

Learn to be authentic. Avoid talking from your head only. Speak also from your heart, from love and goodwill—heart-to-heart. There is a feelable energy when you do this. Reach in and see their world through the eyes of compassion, kindness, and fairness. Learning to see others in this way releases the potential that is in them—and you as well. Enter into a new awareness of the marvelous potential in each person. This is how we become vessels of light.

Be fully present

Do not fall into this trap: while with someone you are in reality online with your friends. No one is that important. People you are with expect your attention, your respect. They want to feel that you value them. It disrespects my time and offends my presence when someone is always checking their phone or wants to show me pictures or videos that are meaningless to me. What's the point of socializing when someone is reading you their Facebook postings and text messages? I refuse invitations from some people because I can count on them doing this. It's bad manners. We need to stop this lack of respect. Be with others as you want them to be with you.

Prepare to be with others

Here is an exercise that may seem difficult at first, but which will become natural when you recognize how valuable it is. When you will be with others, prepare the way by asking for harmony to prevail. It can be a request like, *Heavenly Father, please prepare the situation, guide me, and let harmony prevail among us.*

Then when with someone do your best to focus your heart-love and see it entering into them. Wish them goodness. Your intention will do more than you realize for they will receive in spirit the energy of your care and concern. According to their freedom from negativity will they respond and there will be a successful outcome of being together.

Joy and relationships

Fellowship improves when others feel you are happy. They sense your security and contentment and want to be around you.

We have been conditioned by rampant materialism to look outwardly for happiness. But that is not how it works. It is your inner life that gladdens and makes you confident in yourself and with others. How can someone feel safe with you if you're dissatisfied and unhappy with yourself? How can you have a wholesome relationship when deep wounds fester and cast shadows on everything you do?

Life is meant to be enjoyed, not a burden of sorrow filled days that so many expect. It is not! The universe is friendly and the angels are on your side. Believe that you are designed to be a creative, fulfilled, and happy human being. And then go about your day doing things you enjoy, activities that gladden your heart. This increases and reinforces your capacity to be joyful.

Begin your day with this attitude, *I am here to enjoy life*. Focus on the energy contained in the word "joy." Give it a try and see if it helps you hold onto that attitude during the day. It will become yours over time through the experience of living.

Your physical body needs joy to be at its peak. "A merry heart does good like a medicine: but a broken spirit dries the bones" (Proverbs 17:22). It invites a spiritual frequency of contentment and peace. Outward cheerfulness may wane at times, but you are left with steadfast peace and contentment. Not a bad way to live, wouldn't you say?

Difficult people

I stay away when I am not comfortable with someone, when there's something about them that doesn't feel right. Why I feel that way is eventually revealed. Some people are best loved from a distance. Don't waste your energy focusing on their negative behavior. To do so is to get sucked in and descend to their lower level of vibration. Being emotionally mature is not allowing others to steal your peace. Remember that misery loves company, but it doesn't have to be yours. It is harmful to your mental, emotional, and physical health. All you owe anyone is love, even it's from a distance. I will not give anyone the right to annoy me or disturb my peace. I remain in control of my life.

That's why you have intuition, the connection to your higher mind where your divine Spirit dwells. He signals when something isn't right and tells you how to behave.

The question remains, how do you deal with situations in which you are uncomfortable or you feel people are behaving badly? First of all, don't judge and look down your nose on them; they'll feel it. Instead try to enter into their lives; be empathic and compassionate; we all have problems that we don't handle well. Love the person and not the behavior. That's how you treat someone with respect. They will feel your concern and it will draw the best from them—or at least avoid the worst.

It will help you immensely if you would reach up to your higher consciousness. It is here that your indwelling Spirit collaborates with your human mind. You will avoid reacting with uncontrolled emotions and instead make decisions that bring out the best.

What is the purpose of strong emotions, like being angry with someone? Is it wrong to have these feelings? What do you do with them? Sound relationships require self-control. You can't be beating someone over the head (hopefully figuratively) and expect to get the best from them. Nevertheless, there is a place for righteous anger; be sure you know the difference. Here's one way you can tell: after you express your strong feelings, they leave and you're at peace with yourself. But if they linger and keep bothering you, that's self out of control.

61

As you come to rely on your intuition, you become confident that your feelings are not based on your lower emotions but on a reality that transcends them. It will dramatically improve your relationships and help others improve their lives.

Criticism and grudges

A study showed that people who are always criticizing end up molding negative patterns into their minds. Fortunately, it also works in the reverse: people who make it a lifestyle of showing gratitude tend to be healthier, have positive emotions, deal with adversity better, and have enduring relationships. The silver lining of moving from criticism into gratitude is twofold: first, you're wiring your mind for positivity; and second, you're helping your body become healthier.

We disapprove of people based on the faults and mistakes we think we see. But are they the truth of the matter? How often do we judge a situation that turns out to be different than it appeared? What a waste of our mental and emotional energy when we're wrong about someone's behavior.

Fortunately, as we mature spiritually we learn not to criticize, condemn, complain, and hold grudges. When we become emotionally mature we don't go through life reacting to everyone's behavior. Don't give anyone the power to deflect you from your destiny. Keep your purpose in life foremost. Be the thermostat and not the thermometer.

You cannot have a good relationship if you hold a grudge or are always criticizing. Sounds obvious, doesn't it? But what if you can't help yourself? There is a surefire remedy, but you may not like the medicine. But here's the therapy if you're serious about it. Pray for that person *every* day. And the next part is where it gets more difficult: tell them you are praying for them, and then be in their company. You'll see what a wonderful change it makes in you. You will feel good about yourself.

Changing roles

You grow in stages, and in each stage do 100%. That means being untiring, persevering, and patient with yourself as you fulfill that portion of your life. I know by giving it my all that I will be prepared when ready for my next stage. Because you give it your all there's no need to return to where you once were and live in the past.

In life nothing is permanent, everything is temporary and changing. Because I used to do something, don't expect me to keep doing it, like someone's idea of how I should be a mother at this time of my life. Someone mentioned in my social media about being a grandmother. I said, "I wasn't born to be a grandmother." Wow! She went nuts. "How can you say that!?" Here's how. There's a big difference between having grandchildren and being a grandmother. In my culture in Venezuela, grandmothers take care of their children's children, and so my grandmother raised me. My mother had her work to do and other things. That's how it is in Latin America.

I'm in America now. I don't want to raise my daughter's children. I can have grandchildren and not be a grandmother. You could see why I said, I wasn't born to be a grandmother.

So what's the conclusion of all this? Know when it's time to change and don't allow anyone to tell you differently.

Your health affects relationships

For the most part relationships take place beyond the body, in mind and spirit. But they do depend on your physical health and well-being. If you are hurting or unhappy with how you look, it will affect how you come across to people. Think back when you snapped at someone because you weren't feeling well. Or someone let you have it because they couldn't take the pain.

Another reason to look your best is so people feel good when they see you. How are they going to feel if they see an old hag or someone who looks sick all the time? Do you think they'll say, *She makes me feel good; I can't wait to be around her?*

All this is to say that it's important to work on your body and your health if you want good relationships. It's part of the relationship package.

Soul stages of relationship

Know where you stand with others. This way you have no illusions; you know who you are dealing with and how best to go about it.

These are five levels of soul relationship:[5]

1. A soul relationship which is dominated by kindness, compassion, understanding, and love—values that reflect the highest of ideals.
2. Two people have embarked upon a purposeful relationship and are eager to improve it. It's a constant struggle but they are determined and doing their best.
3. People haven't reached the place where they generally agree about things. They do not yet understand and accept each another. This stage comes before a meaningful relationship.
4. This level of relationship involves strangers and acquaintances. There may be kindness but soul love is not present.
5. On this lowest level a person is so undeveloped that he is incapable of having a relationship.

---

[5] Relationship. (5.14.2000). Daynal Institute.
http://nordan.daynal.org/wiki/index.php?title=2000-05-14-Babies,_Adjusters#Relationship

IN SUMMARY

I came across this guidance about relationships and thought it said well what I'm trying to get across. So here it is (slightly edited):[6]

It is important that you look around and include others in your life, for only then are you truly alive. It is only when you share your life with others that your life begins to mean something. Hiding yourself and your feelings will not bring joy to your life whereas opening up and sharing yourself greatly improves happiness.

It is up to you to socialize with those who inhabit this planet with you. It is up to you to cultivate relationships with them so they may flourish, bloom, and live. It is up to you to open up and let others into your life. It is up to you to bring joy into their lives. It is up to you to make an everlasting impact on this world.

You have free will to create your own reality. You have the power to imagine and create. You have the knowledge and the gift to give love to the world and have the world love you back. It will always be your choice.

This is a very simple lesson to learn. It is not difficult to understand but for some it is difficult to execute. They blame life for the circumstances they are in. Sometimes they blame God for the conditions in which they find themselves. But it is not so. We all make our own decisions, we all make our own choices, we all choose to be where we are (whether it seems so or not). You choose who you want to be, you choose where you want to be, and you choose the spiritual level you are at.

Remember, with each level of advancement you will have greater challenges. Be prepared, for if you choose a life of spirituality you choose a life of challenges.

---

[6] Teacher JarEl. Daynal Institute. (June 13, 2005). See Yourself Through Eyes of Others.
http://www.nordan.daynal.org/wiki/index.php?title=2005-06-13-See_Yourself_Through_Eyes_of_Others

AFTERWORD

Dr. josefina's Way

There is an art to relationships which must be learned. I've shared some of the things that work for me. While the principles are the same for all of us, being unique, you can't live as I do. Learn what works for you; otherwise you can't be true to yourself.

You have opportunity every day to experiment and do your best to develop relationship skills. Of course it is more than technique. It is love in action, the desire to do good to others, without which nothing else really matters.

Be patient with yourself when you make mistakes. That's how we learn. Your day-by-day effort to become a loving person is more important than the results. Be assured that learning every day how best to be to others will eventually yield the fruits of the spirit in your life. People will want to be in your company. And you will be honored to share your life with them.

Be always mindful: RELATIONSHIP ABOVE ALL.

QUESTIONS FOR YOU TO ANSWER

I asked for suggestions about this book. Here are some questions I received. Rather than me answering them, it will be educational to reflect on what you have read and answer them yourself. You might want to share them with others and see what you come up with. In the multitude of counsel there is wisdom.

If you like, post the question and your answer on my Facebook page (www.facebook.com/drjosefina). I would like to hear what you have to say and I'm sure others would like to know your thoughts as well.

Sometimes I just want to be by myself but feel obligated to be with someone. What are the right reasons for being alone and the wrong reasons for being with someone?

My parents have a lot to say about my relationship with my husband. I feel they're trying to control how I live with him. What is the best way to deal with this?

My boyfriend and I actively work out. We want to support each other but our fitness levels are different. For example, when we sign up for 5K events, he prefers to run but I would rather walk because I'm not as fit as him and I'm afraid of hurting my knees. He knows this and he walks to be supportive of me. Should I show my support by encouraging him to go ahead and run, or just thank him for being supportive and walking with me?

How do you determine if a relationship interferes with or helps your lifestyle?

What should you do when your expectations of a relationship differ?

How does menopause affect relationships? What can you do about it?

I was with a man who is jealous of my "ME" time at the gym. He would come to be with me but would stay right on top me so I had no time to talk to anyone else. I felt like I couldn't breathe. I feel this is my time to work hard, challenge myself, and get stronger. He says that I have no time to think about anything except looking and feeling great. What do you think?

I lost my husband and am a widow now. When I'm ready for another relationship, is it best to find someone who eats healthy and exercises daily? Or maybe that's just my thing and it doesn't matter? Seems it would be easier if we had similar lifestyles?

Would you comment on how society looks at and treats women after they reach 50. It seems we contribute to the problem, that we are our own enemy.

Made in the USA
Middletown, DE
01 August 2018